ACTORS ABOUT ACTING, LOVING, LIVING, LIFE

COMPILED BY
DAVID STEELE TURNER

STANYAN BOOKS

RANDOM HOUSE

A Stanyan book
Published by Stanyan Books,
8721 Sunset Blvd., Suite C
Hollywood, California 90069,
and by Random House, Inc.
201 East 50th Street,
New York, N.Y. 10022

Printed in U.S.A.

Designed by Hy Fujita

Library of Congress Catalog
Card Number: 79-182686

ISBN: 0-394-48060-0

ACTORS ABOUT ACTING, LOVING, LIVING, LIFE

I often think my life has been a failure. But whenever I drop into a theater and hear women laughing at one of my films, I think, well, if I brightened their day before they went home and did the dishes, maybe my life wasn't wasted after all.

— Cary Grant

They come for you in the morning in a limousine; they take you to the studio; they stick a pretty girl in your arms; sometimes they earn something off you and give you some of the profits. They call that a profession? — come on!

— Marcello Mastroianni

It isn't what I do, but how I do it.
It isn't what I say, but how I say it —
and how I look when I do and say it.

— Mae West

Actors have a bad handle on the world. I'll tell you, in my own mind, I'm not sure acting is a thing for a grown man to be doing.

— Steve McQueen

Like all actresses, I'm a shattered personality, with lots and lots of people inside me crying to get out . . .

— Raquel Welch

I was much, much too successful much too soon. I was a star at 21. I was the youngest person to ever win the *Tony.* Acting was my whole life. I was THE actress. Nothing else mattered. No outside relationship was important. I threw my whole life into everything I did. If that sounds arrogant, you have to be arrogant to get up there night after night and tell people: "Love me, love me, love me!" . . .

— Elizabeth Ashley

No actor—I don't care whether he's Richard Burton or Laurence Olivier—can act pain. You have to actually suffer it to make it look authentic.

— Richard Harris

I got all the schooling any actress needs. That is, I learned to write enough to sign contracts.

— Hermione Gingold

If I weren't doing what I'm doing now, the actress thing, the star business if you want to call it that, whatever it is, I'd be in an asylum. I'm sure of it.

— Mia Farrow

They can stop hiring this old horse and put him out to pasture—but I'll never go of my own accord.

— John Wayne

I like to work in Hollywood, but I don't like to live there. I'm too young to die.

— Claire Bloom

Looking back, I can't believe some of the things they got me to do. Arriving at a premiere in a car with two huge dogs next to me—dressing up as Harlow to go across the Atlantic on the Queen Mary . . . In the end it led to a kind of nervous breakdown. When I came out of it I realized I was faced with two choices: the way out that Marilyn Monroe took, or to run away.
I just ran.

— ***Carroll Baker***

Method acting? There are quite a few methods. Mine involves a lot of talent, a glass, and some cracked ice.

— ***John Barrymore***

This isn't exactly a stable business. It's like trying to stand up in a canoe with your pants down.

— ***Cliff Robertson***

What would I tell a young actress starting out today? Take care of your health. Deny yourself fun like you'll never know. And when you make a picture, you have to say, "This is all I do." Pretty bloody boring, if you think about it.

— ***Bette Davis***

To survive in this business, you need a short memory and the constitution of an ox.

— ***Ingrid Bergman***

The main thing about acting is luck: to be born with the proper set of shoulders; to be as enormous as John Wayne; to be beautifully ugly, as Humphrey Bogart was; as short, squat and vital as Jimmy Cagney; as solid as Eddie Robinson. Most importantly, you must have that particular compulsion for an audience, and it is productive if you can tell the imagination of that audience.

— ***Richard Burton***

I always said I would never get married until someone gave me one good reason for marriage, aside from the social, conventional one. Nobody ever did, but I married anyway, for social, conventional reasons—and my father.

— Jane Fonda

You know why I've been married so many times? Take the seven men. I could have lived with any of them, other than the father of my daughter, without that piece of paper. But I want it right on the table; I want it legal. I gotta marry 'em. Better I shouldn't, maybe, but I did.

— Lana Turner

I always said I won't marry until I go to Japan and see the beautiful women there. I've been to Japan now and I have to have another excuse.

— Maximilian Schell

I'm exactly like the girl I play in *Company*—I'm terrified of marriage. Because my own experience was so painful. I suppose it's possible to discover yourself in a marriage but it's better to know yourself beforehand. Or else you don't understand why until it's too late.

— Beth Howland

Marriage is just not something you pick up and do when it's convenient. It's a responsibility . . . It's very hard. Just because so many people are doing it doesn't mean they're doing it well. They're doing it bloody awful.

— Elizabeth Ashley

In California, I find people have the same psychology about marriage as they have about buying a house. They buy a house to live in five years and then get another one. When they go into a house, they're already thinking of the next one.

— Connie Stevens

Acting is agony for me. It's wonderful to have done a film, but while I'm making it I feel like I'm diving into cold water every time I step in front of the camera.

— Ursula Theiss

One of the most destructive things in my life was the kind of parts I played in pictures. I studied Shakespeare and the classics, and I end up shooting Joan Crawford and killing a horse that Elizabeth Taylor was in love with. I'm serious. I played the worst harridans, the most hard-bitten women, the absolute heavies, and it just about did me in.

— Mercedes McCambridge

Working in the theater you see few people and they are always the same. After I went to Albania people said, "Why on earth did you do that?" I couldn't very well say, "To get away from you," but there it was . . .

— Peter Ustinov

We did *Long Day's Journey* for two years—that was enough! I've had the theater. It becomes a damn bore night after night.

—Fredric March

They throw that word 'star' at you loosely, and they take it away loosely if your pictures flop. *You* take the responsibility for *their* crappy movie, that's all it means.

—Robert Redford

I can see the difficulties of making a movie. Directors and producers have to put up with a lot of rubbish from temperamental actors.

—Richard Harris

I can look at all my movies and tell you which ones I made while betting heavy on the horses. I always had one ear off-stage, listening for the call from the bookie.

—Walter Matthau

The real, *real* reason I like to be in movies is because it's an easy place to have my hems done. There's always a seamstress on the set. And if you break a chair, they can fix it—they have people who do everything. Chair people, hem people.

— Barbra Streisand

I played Patton because I liked the man . . . he was an individual. That's what's most important to me today—when everybody else around seems to be some kind of damn ostrich.

— George C. Scott

Talkative theatergoers try to be clever instead of watching me be clever.

— Noel Coward

The Oscar means one thing—an added million dollar gross to the picture. It has nothing to do with "acclaim of your peers." It's a big publicity contest . . . Oh, the voting is legitimate, but there's the sentimentality. One year when I was a candidate, when Elizabeth Taylor got a hole in her throat, I canceled my plane.

— Shirley MacLaine

Nobody can be exactly like me. Sometimes even I have trouble doing it.

— Tallulah Bankhead

Life is a constant fight, but beautiful. You fight every day for what you believe, but it is worth it. It is all too short, anyway. It is a race run so fast it is a shame . . . I want to do only the things I believe in deeply, so that I can look in the mirror at my face and not be ashamed.

— Alain Delon

We're all searching for paradise, but it's something you remember having once—and never realizing you had it then.

— Richard Harris

Storms come, houses are wiped out, people drown, but every last little palm is there after the storm. Man is always saying, "I will overwhelm." Why can't he bend like the little palms? And rise again. Isn't that better than being broken and washed away?

— Kim Novak

Youth always accuses the generations ahead of them of being intolerant. There's nothing more intolerant than youth. Young people have lots of knowledge crammed into them now. But they can't assess it—that's wisdom.

— ***Roger Moore***

It's the ones you can call up at four a.m. who matter.

— ***Marlene Dietrich***

Today, there is too much concentration on externals. The things that really count are the ones that stay with you when your flamboyant period of youth has passed. The older women who do not realize this have sad-looking faces because the things they depended on are no longer there. They make an effort to appear young, but what imbalance there is when not a line of living is left in the face and their eyes are old, old.

— ***Dana Wynter***

You may as well stay home and listen to a recording as watch a dark-suited piano player.

— Liberace

I go off stage and always return after counting to four. Some comedians count to seven, but I won't do that. I tried it once, and when I came back the busboys were clearing off the tables.

— Bob Newhart

I've spent my life in the saddle, and it's darned uncomfortable. But with a face like mine, it's inevitable.

— Lee Marvin

Ho-ho, I said to him (Patrick Curtis, her mentor and erstwhile lover). You look like a nasty Svengali. Aren't I glad you pulled me out of the gutter when I was just lying there with no teeth and flat as a board!

— Raquel Welch

My voice is not a put-on. I was already singing bass when I was in the fourth grade.

— ***Carol Channing***

Acting is a child's prerogative. Children are born to act. Usually, people grow up and out of it. Actors always seem to me people who never did quite grow out of it.

— ***Joanne Woodward***

When I began in the theater, I thought I was an introvert in a field of extroverts. But they're all terrified, frightened, insecure people who have found this remarkable outlet of playing all these characters who are not themselves.

— ***Robert Young***

As soon as they say "Action," I can smell in the first two seconds whether I am going to get on the wave or not. And if you don't get on, you have this disastrous feeling. I can tell you—it's like love without climax.

— ***Genevieve Bujold***

They say I am always playing myself. I have played all these different parts—but of course I am always myself! In every character. What else is a star? My God! Bernhardt—the essence of Bernhardt was always there. Miss Hayes, Miss Cornell, Mr. Tracy, Mr. Gable —the same. The essence is always there.

— Bette Davis

I hope the way I play Mame she's more than just a song and dance. She's all the women I've played. I'm like a sponge. Everything I see is ducated away in my pores. I've known a lot of Mames in my day and underneath they all cry, "Need me." It's taken me forty-one years, but I've finally found a role that's the sum total of everything I know and everybody's digging me for the first time.

— Angela Lansbury

Basically, there are two types of heroes. One of them has the world against him . . . and everyone says that's great acting. The other, the romantic action type, has the most absurd dialogue and situations. The job then is keeping the grin off your face. That's acting, too, isn't it?

— Roger Moore

It's hard to make the unbelievable believable, and that's what we have to do. It's also hard not to break up while you're doing it. When Herbert Marshall and I were filming *The Fly*, we had to do one of the scenes back to back, because every time we looked at each other we fell apart. It was about this fly, you see, with a human head.
Well, I *ask* you.

— Vincent Price

What is the main problem of the actor? It is to keep the audience awake, and not let them go to sleep, then wake up and go home feeling they've wasted their money.

— Sir Laurence Olivier

You can sum up my life and my acting in one sentence: "I want to play all the strings in the bow, because I want to find out how many strings there are . . ."

— ***Richard Harris***

I'm often asked, "Why have you stayed in pictures so long? You're not a leading man, you're not a pretty fellow, you're not a star. Why?" Is it possible that I'm a good actor?

— ***Anthony Quinn***

I don't think it's necessary for talented people to show their bodies on the screen . . . I think it will be exciting some day if a picture begins with a nude person who's putting his clothes on, and keeps them on for the rest of the picture.

— ***Danny Thomas***

A stageful of very attractive young people undressed could be pleasant, but I think it rather holds up the action.

— ***Noel Coward***

I've no objection to watching naked bodies on the stage, but they must be beautiful. And usually those with really beautiful bodies can't act. So what's the point?

— John Gielgud

What bothers me about some of this new stuff is it doesn't give young actors the kind of training they should have. Hell, *anybody* can stand naked in front of an audience and shout Holy! Holy! But *anybody* can't perform Shakespeare or Shaw or Neil Simon.

— Robert Ryan

Everybody's taking their clothes off but me. You'll never catch me in the buff, kiddo.

— Lucille Ball

In New York I went to see a play, *Geese*, in which the cast strip naked. I wanted to see if one acts any better with one's clothes off. After seeing it, I decided they couldn't act even with their clothes on. But I had to see it. It is theater.

— Rex Harrison

All through an actor's life, failure is snapping at his heels like a giant mongrel dog. But because conceit is an actor's courage, he refuses to recognize that dog as anything more than a puppy who really can't harm him. Without conceit, an actor couldn't get anywhere; and maybe this applies to anyone who wants to get to the top in any profession.

— Jackie Gleason

It's painful for me to act—sheer hell while I'm doing it. I live a role . . . for three months, and every day is agony. I can never hang a part up on a peg when I go home.

— Peter O'Toole

The hardest thing about being a star is that you feel one step apart from humanity. You walk into a restaurant and get the best table—that's beautiful. But to walk down the street and not be able to be part of the crowd—man, that can really drive you up the wall!

— Stuart Whitman

All actors feel insecure at times . . . You're on top one minute and the next minute—zappo! It's a cruel and capricious profession and you've got *nothing* to fall back on. So actors find shields to hide from their insecurity and pain. Sometimes mine is a bottle.

— *George C. Scott*

It's very hard for an actress . . . to be a star. When it happens, it's difficult to believe. Then you're expected to live up to what people expect of you as a star. The battle against you by yourself is endless.

— *Angela Lansbury*

The only time I'm happy is when I'm doing absolutely nothing. When I work I vomit all the time. I know nothing about acting so I have one rule—trust the director and give him heart and soul. And nothing else.

— *Ava Gardner*

Acting is a way to overcome your own inhibitions and shyness. The writer creates a strong, confident personality, and that's what you become—unfortunately, only for the moment.

— Shirley Booth

Technique is when you can look at the rushes and say to yourself that you've maintained the mood of the character for three days before the camera, while you yourself have felt three different ways.

— Lee Remick

I get the greatest kind of soaring feeling from this work (in *Applause*). . . . You get the feeling that you're making good use of yourself, and nothing makes you feel better than that . . . It's exhilarating, and it's coming at such a crucial time for me . . . It's like a second chance . . . I'm counting on this for a lot because, believe me, I'm *due.* I'm *overdue.*

— Lauren Bacall

I am very vulnerable. It is enough for me while I work, to spot a member of the crew who is indifferent. Maybe he yawns, or just couldn't care less. It bothers me. I will do the scene next time doing my best to involve him. In other words, I need reassurance all the time, as all of us do.

— Sophia Loren

The secret of staying fresh in a show is to remember that the audience you're playing for that night has never seen it before.

— Danny Kaye

The stage takes more from your life in three hours of work than one whole day in the film studio. On stage, you are a prisoner, even though it is a lovely prison.

— Danielle Darrieux

I like to work. Inactivity is one of the great indignities of life. Through inactivity, people lose their self-respect, their integrity. The need to work is always there, bugging me.

— Joan Crawford

What can you tell about happiness? But about sadness there is much to say. It is real and more interesting than gaiety.

— Charles Aznavour

It would be a waste of time to attain total sanity. I don't even have an image of sanity. It's a mistake to have one. This madness isn't confined to actors and show business. Plumbing contractors and insurance salesmen, for instance, are faking sanity. The whole world is a collective maniac acting out a charade or pretending to an image of sanity.

— John Astin

In my office in Paris, I have a photograph of the earth taken from the moon . . . It helps me have the right values. I may be a great big movie star down here, but from up there I am nothing, and we are all nothing.

— Alain Delon

It is character, individuality, inner beauty—call it what you like—that makes a person memorable. Sometimes, too much accent is placed on what you want people to see and not enough on what you want them to feel.

— ***Nancy Kovack***

The days in my life that stand out most vividly are the days I've learned something. There is a feeling I get—it's so exciting I can't describe it . . . All the good things in life come hard; but wisdom is the hardest to come by.

— ***Lucille Ball***

In an affair you don't have to make the effort to understand. You can exist on fun and games—playing house. But in a marriage if you do that you're walking out on some pretty brutal commitments. And maybe even a dream or two.

— ***Charles Braswell***

There are so many things happening, so many things to learn, to be conscious of—it's immoral to hide yourself in a world of drugs.

— ***Geraldine Chaplin***

Every bride should know the answer to this important question: "Do I care for him enough to put his interests first, to find pleasure in pleasing him?" Too many girls think about what they are going to receive rather than what they are going to give . . . It's a case that when love flows thick, faults flow thin.

— Barbara Bain

Everybody's afraid. Couples who've been married for thirty years wake up in a cold sweat . . . I sometimes wonder if some of my married friends don't ask me to come around—alone—to sing for my supper and give 'em a lot of laughs —so they won't have to cope with each other.

— Elaine Stritch

You know what my personal image of marriage is? Lying on our bed Sunday morning with the Times spread out and the radio playing and the kids squealing and laughing in the pillows with us. Somebody called marriage 'the density of living.' I think that's a perfect description, don't you?

— Barbara Barrie

Being a comedian is like being a con man. You have to make 'em like you before you can fool 'em.

—Flip Wilson

Laughter is much more important than applause. Applause is almost a duty. Laughter is a reward. Laughter means they trust and like you.

—Carol Channing

When a radio comedian's program is finally finished it slinks down Memory Lane into the limbo of yesterday's happy hours. All that the comedian has to show for his years of work and aggravation is the echo of forgotten laughter.

—Fred Allen

I miss nightclubs—as much as possible.

— Peter Lind Hayes

Having been made a Dame (by the Queen) has made a slight difference in my life. I find myself wearing gloves more often.

— Dame Judith Anderson

I am terribly lazy. That's why I love being in movies. I'm performing all over the world—while I'm home taking a bath.

— Barbra Streisand

Today, sex comes from the personality and how you look at a man. The bust is not so important any more. But, of course, I'm not bad.

— Gina Lollobrigida

I don't want my kids to grow up believing that there is nothing destructive in the world. I want them to know that there is good and bad in the world, that you can be hurt physically, that guns can kill you, that drugs are bad for you, that not everyone means well.

— ***Chuck Connors***

It's awful being an actress, because you're up one minute, down the next. Everybody likes you when they want you, then they don't want you and they couldn't care less if you die. But Hollywood is changing. Stupid talk like "Snow pictures don't make money," or "You can't put love in the title, it won't sell," is passé. Maybe it's heresy for me to say this, but stars shouldn't matter.

— ***Jane Fonda***

Why should anybody care about what any movie star has to say? A movie star is nothing important. Freud, Gandhi, Marx—these people are important. But movie acting is just dull, boring, childish work . . . movie stars are nothing as actors . . . I guess Garbo was the last one who had it.

— ***Marlon Brando***

As for making movies, who can act at eight o'clock in the morning? Let's face it!

— ***John Carradine***

I absolutely adore movies. Even bad ones. I don't like pretentious ones, but a good bad movie, you must admit, is great.

— ***Roddy McDowall***

. . . when you're making a film you do one or two scenes a day, usually out of sequence . . . bits, 30 seconds at a time, over a six-week period. Then the director puts it together, and you may turn out just fine. But no matter how many awards you win for that picture, you have no recollection of ever creating the character.

— ***Henry Fonda***

An actor can survive a bad play, particularly if his performance is well received. But a bad movie . . .

— ***Art Carney***

I think some of the people who go to the movies are more intelligent than the people who make them.

— Rod Steiger

I am happy for Goldie Hawn (Oscar winner for best supporting actress) but also a little sad. She will always miss that special enjoyment of getting one after years of *working* for it. That she will regret. You saw how John Wayne had to brush away a tear. I don't think Goldie would have been crying.

— Ingrid Bergman

I'm tired of playing the lecherous, middle-aged chap who is forever vaulting the generation gap.

— James Mason

There must be something wrong with a group (the Motion Picture Academy) that hands out awards and has to send telegrams saying, please come.

— Paul Newman

In our day, stars had it lucky. The studios built our careers with care and bought vehicles or created them especially for us. Today's stars must take what comes to them. And if they make the wrong choices, they're dead.

— ***Bette Davis***

I don't know whether they'll sell the studios, but it looks that way. And it's sad. The other day I said to this darling little driver I have at MGM, "Do you want to go somewhere with me?" We toured the lot, and I saw the house Scarlett lived in. I saw the little cottage Garbo lived in. I saw the house Andy Hardy lived in. And I cried. . . .

— ***Anne Jackson***

Elation, that's what I feel. Just think, I no longer need worry how I feel physically, whether my voice is right, whether my costume is secure, whether I'm going to trip or make a false move. I have worried about these things, feared these things for as long as I can remember . . . Now I'm free of them . . .

— ***Helen Hayes***
(after her last stage appearance)

I prefer the theater to motion pictures and Hollywood doesn't seem a bit upset about it. I discovered that in the theater you don't have to look like Liz Taylor to get the guy at the end of the show.

— Elaine Stritch

The stage is vital to an actor. On the stage, a performance is all yours. Nobody can edit you or cut you out. Actors need the stage for the rejuvenation of their abilities and equipment.

— Arthur O'Connell

Playwrights are like men who have been dining a month in an Indian restaurant. After eating curry night after night, they deny the existence of asparagus.

— Peter Ustinov

A great deal of it (theater) should be sheer enjoyment, not always having problems bashed into your head.

— Cyril Ritchard

Name me one character in literature or drama who can't be described as neurotic. . . . We wouldn't want to know the people we go to see on the stage. How would you like to have Medea for dinner? Or Macbeth slurping your soup? Or Oedipus with his bloody, blinded eyes dripping all over your tablecloth?

— ***Geraldine Page***

There is an audience for every play; it's just that sometimes it can't wait long enough to find it.

— ***Shirley Booth***

Playing one character over and over again is not my notion of being an actor. It's like a painter having a five-year contract with the Hilton Hotel chain. He paints the same picture in every room of every hotel for five years. He will make a lot of money. But what kind of satisfaction would that be for a genuine painter?

— ***Leslie Nielsen***

Americans playing Shakespeare are really ridiculous.

— ***Glenn Ford***

For some dancers, being on stage doesn't matter so much—their heartbeat doesn't change . . . But for me, just standing in the wings before going on, I am already exhausted, dead . . . It's extraordinary how terrified I am.

— ***Rudolf Nureyev***

Life is a cycle, and mime is particularly suitable for showing fluidity, transformation, metamorphosis. Words can keep people apart; mime can be a bridge between them.

— ***Marcel Marceau***

When you're young, you look for the romance in acting. You set out to slay the dragon. . . . It isn't until later, much later, when you're in it and it's too late to get out, that the romance flies out the window.

— ***Lee J. Cobb***

I always have to be working hard at something. I'm kind of like the old-time farm women. You know, drop the baby and pick up the plow.

— Edie Adams

Really, I'm rather square. But it's the squares who carry the burden of the world, and the bores who become heroes.

— Katharine Hepburn

I was a rebel, and my idea of expressing this was to look a mess. Our whole group tried to shock people by going around like the hippies do today, but there was no name for us. We were really conforming, and one only sees this with the eyes of maturity.

— Joanne Woodward

Even when I was single, I owned homes and gardens. I buy beauty where other women buy jewels . . . Land is security to me. I need gardens that are mine to walk on . . .

— Merle Oberon

The happiest time of my life was when I was laying bricks.

— George C. Scott

I've worked with a lot of great glamorous girls in movies and the theater. And I'll admit, I've often thought it would be wonderful to be a femme fatale. But then I'd always come back to thinking that if they only had what I've had—a family, real love, an anchor—they would have been so much happier during all the hours when the marquees and the footlights are dark.

— Eve Arden

Actors have ego problems, and acting gives them a release for those problems. Take me. I was shy, felt inferior, thought everybody was better than I was. When I acted, I wasn't Michael Ansara alone. I was Michael Ansara and a great talent. I was announcing, "Look at me. I'm good. I'm great." It was making people admire and love me. Some actors are exceptions to the rule. But I haven't met any.

— Michael Ansara

People like to think of you as that great superhuman figure on the screen doing all those giant things. In the end, a lot of actors get to thinking they are like that. First we've got to learn to be human beings—we mustn't just be our profession.

— James Coburn

Good God, some of the new young actors say they don't know whether they want to be actors or not! I cannot understand this. To me, it is like saying you can't make up your mind whether or not you love a certain woman. If you don't, then take a walk. In acting, as in love, there is no place for indifference.

— Trevor Howard

For a famous actor, a famous politician or writer, everybody puts on an act for you because you're famous. Nobody is, strictly speaking, himself any more. So apart from the fact you yourself are not behaving normally because you're well known, others don't behave normally either, for the same reason. So you lose touch with reality.

— Richard Burton

People always ask me the most ridiculous questions. They want to know, "How do you approach a role?" Well, I don't know. I approach it by first saying yes, then getting on with the bloody thing.

— Dame Edith Evans

I have never regretted the choice of any parts I have done. Because you get involved in the part, you grow to love the character, and you can never regret something you love.

— Rex Harrison

I started out in vaudeville, and vaudeville died. I hit the burlesque houses, and they padlocked 'em. I tried radio, and you know what happened to radio. Then live TV, and it vanished. Now that I've finally got a toehold in movies, look what's happening to them.

— Jack Albertson

Isn't it sad? Children are so alive and awake and they listen and see and touch and experience so fully. Then they grow up and become dead. They've stopped changing; they've decided, "This is what I am," and that's death. Things should be in perpetual change.

— Jane Fonda

You must never lose the excitement of life.

— Jack Benny

As a completely normal woman, I enjoy being in the nude. It does to me something as it probably does many other females. Like them, I often feel a vague need for some kind of psychoanalytic treatment; but then, by dropping clothes, I think I drop not merely the so-called moral inhibitions but also a few others which cause me relentless timidity, lack of confidence, inferiority complexes. Stripping means mental recovery—to me in any case.

— Anna Moffo

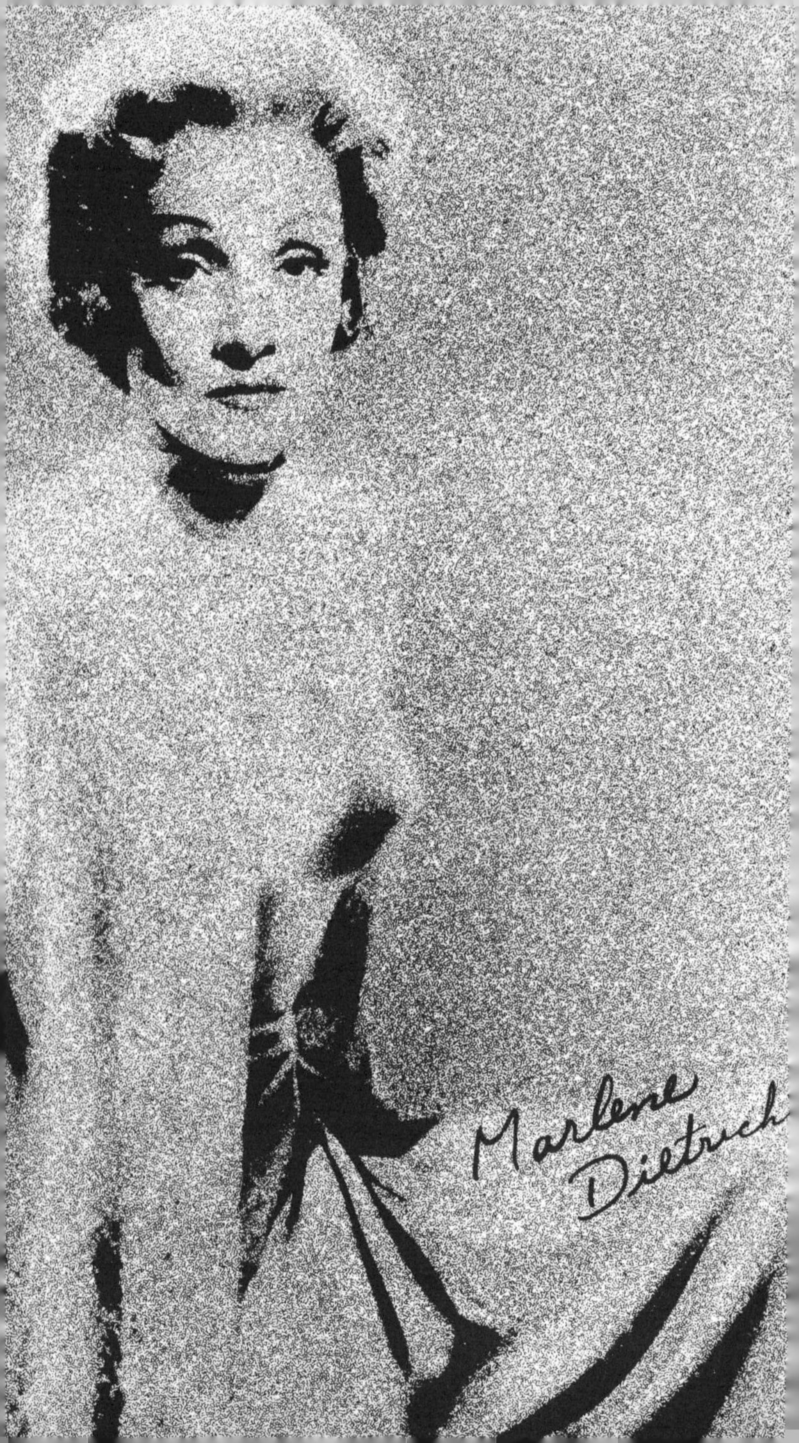
Marlene
Dietrich

I am tired of being called a sexy grandmother. Artur Rubinstein is a great artist, but who gives a damn how many grandchildren *he* has?

— Marlene Dietrich

Traditional marriage is oppressive. Till death do us part in handcuffs. More men are afraid of marriage than women. They're afraid of losing their identities, their sexuality. They're afraid of the divorce and alimony because these days men don't believe that marriage can last. Another reason men are afraid: we women are changing. Dramatically. We expect more of ourselves and more is expected of us.

— Alice Cannon

Unless something comes along that absolutely captivates me, the life of leisure is for me—if you call being married to Richard Burton and the mother of four leisure.

— Elizabeth Taylor

Men who believe in indiscriminate scoring with girls will never find a deep, lasting relationship. Hugh Hefner must be the most anti-female man in America.

— Yvette Mimieux

I'm not so artistic that I despise profit.

— Sir Laurence Olivier

Ninety per cent of the things you do in this business are crap.

— Jack Albertson

I don't know what it is I exude. But whatever it is, it's whatever I am!

— Janet Leigh

What do I want to do? What a dumb question! I'm *doing* it.

— Johnny Carson

A choreographer takes an idea out of his head and transposes it on people's anatomy.

— Gene Kelly

Actors and burglars work better at night.

— ***Sir Cedric Hardwicke***

Every actor in his heart believes everything bad that's printed about him.

— ***Orson Welles***

Retire? I couldn't retire; I just couldn't. I'm too much of a ham.

— ***Jack Benny***

Daddy has never seen anything I've done, but he is the best critic I have. He has taught me how to tear down a character. "Slug your guts out" is his philosophy of acting. Never mind the talent, just work hard.

— ***Geraldine Chaplin***

I would like to be remembered—well, the Mexicans have an expression, feo, fuerte y formal, which means: He was ugly, was strong and had dignity.

— ***John Wayne***

I don't want a quickie love affair with the public. I want to keep working until I end up in the home for old actors with my friends. . . . By the time stars have the part and billing they demand, all they care is how their hair was set and their mouth was shaped the particular year they last worked.

— Lee Grant

An audience identifies with the actors of flesh and blood and heartbeat, as no reader or beholder can identify with even the most artful paragraphs in books or the most inspiring paintings. There, says the watcher, but for some small difference in time or costume or inflections or gait, go I . . . And so, the actor becomes a catalyst; he brings to bright ignition that spark in every human being that longs for the miracle of transformation.

— Edward G. Robinson